RUGBY

Clive Gifford

First published in 2007 by Wayland

Wayland
338 Euston Road
London NW1 3BH

Wayland Australia
Level 17/207 Kent Street
Sydney NSW 2000

Senior Editor: Jennifer Schofield
Designers: Rachel Hamdi and Holly Fulbrook
Illustrators: Ian Thompson and Holly Fulbrook
Picture Researcher: Clive Gifford
Proofreader: Patience Coster

Picture Acknowledgements:
cover, 4, 26, 35 Odd Andersen/AFP/Getty Images; 5, 8 Christophe Simon/AFP/Getty Images;
6 Hulton Archive/Getty Images; 7 Chris McGrath/Getty Images Sport; 9 Peter Muhly/AFP/Getty
Images; 17, 32, 37, 38 David Rogers/Getty Images Sport; 19, 40 Damien Meyer/AFP/Getty
Images; 20 Glyn Kirk/Action Plus; 21 Torsten Blackwood/AFP/Getty Images; 22, 42 William
West/AFP/Getty Images Images; 23 Hachette Childrenren's Books; 39 Jimmy Jeong/Getty
Images Sport; 24, 41Ross Land/Getty Images Sport; 23 Christopher Lee/ Getty Images Sport;
25 Pascal Pavani/AFP/Getty Images; 28 MN Chan/Getty Images Sport; 29 Harry How/Getty
Images Sport; 30 Shaun Botterill/Getty Images Sport; 31 Jiji Press/AFP/ Getty Images Images;
33 Stu Forster/Getty Images Sport; 34 Francois Guillot/AFP/Getty Images; 43 Jean-Pierre
Muller/AFP/Getty Images; 44 Adam Pretty/Getty Images Sport; 44 Oliver Morin/AFP/Getty
Images; 45 David Cannon/Getty Images Sport; 46 Gilbert Rugby

CIP data
Gifford, Clive
   Rugby. - (Inside sport)
   1. Rugby football - Juvenile literature
   I. Title
   796.3'33

ISBN: 978 0 7502 5248 5

Printed in China

Wayland is a division of Hachette Children's Books

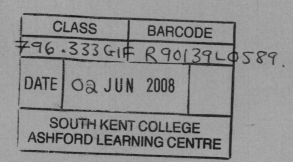

796.333
GIF

X

This book is due for return on or before the last date shown below.

10 NOV 2010

796.333
GIF

R90139L0589.

The Learning Centre
South Kent College
Jemmett Road
Ashford, Kent TN23 2RJ

*Remember you can renew
books over the phone.*

Tel: 01233 655573

CONTENTS

INTRODUCTION

Rugby union is a powerful, exciting team sport which requires strength, courage and large amounts of skill, pace and awareness. Although matches can sometimes turn on a piece of individual brilliance or a single player's mistake, rugby is a team game with all 15 players needing to work as a unit in order for their side to win.

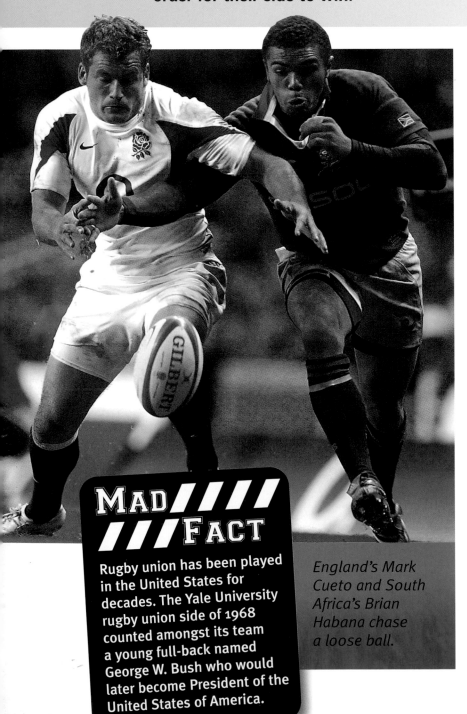

England's Mark Cueto and South Africa's Brian Habana chase a loose ball.

MAD FACT

Rugby union has been played in the United States for decades. The Yale University rugby union side of 1968 counted amongst its team a young full-back named George W. Bush who would later become President of the United States of America.

A Game for Everyone

Rugby can be played by boys and girls, men and women of all abilities. Very young players can play touch or tag rugby where heavy contact and tackling are not allowed. In these scaled-down versions of rugby, the rules are kept simple so that budding players can focus on the basics of passing and catching, running and defending. Veteran sides can see players in their forties and fifties turn out to take part in fun, casual games. While the sport's major teams are based in Europe, Oceania, South Africa and Argentina, rugby is played in over 100 countries. The sport's top competition, the Rugby World Cup, has seen the Ivory Coast, the United States, Uruguay and Japan all appear at the finals.

The Spectators

Rugby may be great to play, but it can also be fascinating to watch. Teams with long histories and explosive players compete in packed stadiums bursting with passionate spectators.

Television and new competitions, such as the World Cups for women and men, have helped boost the sport's popularity in the past 20 years. Only 17,500 people attended the France versus Australia semi-final at the 1987 Rugby World Cup. However, for the 2007 tournament, over 1.6 million match tickets were eagerly snapped up. Total television audiences which were around 300 million for the first tournament had risen to well over 2 billion by the 1999 competition.

Almost 83,000 fans cheer on Australia and England in the final of the 2003 Rugby World Cup. Millions more people tuned in to watch the climax of the match on television.

RUGBY THEN AND NOW

"All matches are drawn after five days or after three days if no goal has been kicked," Rule 39 of Rugby School Rules 1862.

How it All Started

According to legend, in 1823 a pupil, William Webb Ellis, at Rugby School, England, was playing a game of football when he picked up the ball and ran. The sport takes its name from Webb Ellis's school which began forming rules for rugby as did other schools and organizations. Early rugby was unruly with no limits on team numbers. Games could last for a day or more. Rugby union developed out of these and other sets of rules. The International Rugby Board (IRB) – the organization which runs world rugby – was formed in 1886.

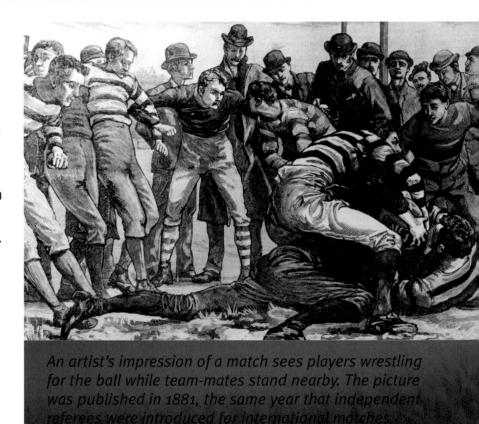

An artist's impression of a match sees players wrestling for the ball while team-mates stand nearby. The picture was published in 1881, the same year that independent referees were introduced for international matches.

Paid to Play

A debate raged about players being paid to play in the late nineteenth century. In 1895 a breakaway group of clubs formed the Northern Football League. Over time, this became the sport of rugby league with its rules developing differently from union. Rugby league now involves 13 players a side with only six players in a scrum, no lineouts and four points for a try. In contrast to professional rugby league, rugby union remained an amateur sport until 1995 when the sport went 'open' and allowed professional players.

Training

With the arrival of professionalism, top rugby footballers became full-time players. Training became longer and more intense. Apart from practising their skills and team play, players now spend much time building their strength in the gym and working on their flexibility, speed and stamina – the ability to work hard for long periods – via running and other exercises. In general, professional players have become faster, fitter and heavier as a result.

Australian Lote Tuqiri and England's Jason Robinson wrestle for the ball during the 2003 Rugby World Cup Final. Both men were former rugby league internationals who changed to rugby union. They also both scored their team's only tries of the match.

Who is...
...Martin Johnson?

Martin Johnson CBE was a tough, uncompromising and inspirational forward who played for England 84 times and led his country to World Cup success in 2003. Playing more than 300 first team matches for Leicester, Johnson's career spanned the amateur and professional eras of rugby union. Before turning professional he worked in a bank. Retiring in 2005, this giant in the lineout and formidable tackler is the only player to captain two British and Irish Lions tours.

Injuries

Although top players are fit and fast, the large amount of rugby they play and the great speed and force of collisions in the tackle have lead to many suffering injuries. Jonny Wilkinson, the player who scored the winning points for England in the 2003 World Cup Final, suffered a glut of injuries that saw him play only a handful of games in the three following seasons. He is not alone. In the 2004/05 season, over 200 English Premiership players suffered injuries which stopped them playing games.

AIM OF THE GAME

Rugby is a 15-a-side sport in which teams run, kick and pass a ball in an attempt to score points. Teams defend by delaying and tackling opponents to stop points being scored against them. The team with the most points when the game ends is the winner.

Clothing and Protection

Rugby is a contact sport and so can be dangerous if players do not play fairly or do not listen to the referee. Clothing is straightforward – shirt, shorts, socks and studded boots. Players also tend to wear additional items to protect themselves. These include shinpads to protect the front of their legs, gumshields and padded headguards called scrum caps. Some also wear upper body protection – a layer of special padding, not more than 1cm thick, worn under their shirt and covering only their shoulder and collar-bone areas.

Game Time

Each full match is played over two halves of 40 minutes each. Knockout competitions, such as the semi-final of a Rugby World Cup, see periods of extra time played if the scores are level at full time.

Australia's Nathan Sharpe, wearing a scrum cap, powers away with the ball during a 2003 Rugby World Cup game.

Who is...

...Brian O'Driscoll?

Brian O'Driscoll is a brilliant attacking player for his club Leinster and has 74 international caps for Ireland, over 30 of them as captain of the side. Playing at centre, he has superb balance, power and pace and had scored 28 tries for his country before the start of the 2007 Six Nations. Made captain of the 2005 British and Irish Lions, O'Driscoll suffered a dislocated shoulder which kept him out of much of that tour. However, he came roaring back and was voted the 2006 Six Nations Player of the Year.

In international matches, the referee who runs the match, pauses the clock for stoppages such as injuries. The two halves of a game are separated by half-time which lasts a maximum of ten minutes. At the start of the second half, the teams switch ends of the pitch.

Starting and Restarting the Game

Each half of the game is started with one team kicking the ball from the middle of the halfway line. The ball must travel forward 10m, stay inside the pitch and none of the kicker's team-mates must be in front of the kicker as the ball is kicked. Unless a foul or infringement occurs, the ball is played until points are scored (see page 10) or the ball goes out of play. If the ball goes out along the sidelines of pitch, a type of throw-in called a lineout (see page 17) is usually used to restart play.

MAD FACT

Basil Maclear first played for Ireland in 1905 and faced the All Blacks and South Africa in his international career. He used to play wearing white gloves!

Brian O'Driscoll dives to score a try for his Irish club side, Leinster.

SCORING POINTS

There are four ways to notch up points in a rugby match: scoring a try and three types of kick – the conversion, the drop kick and the penalty kick. A try is worth five points, a successful penalty or drop kick three, and a conversion kick two points. For any kick to count, the ball must travel over the crossbar and in a line between the two goal posts, or above but in line with them.

Paul Volley celebrates as he scores a try for his English club side, Wasps against Irish team, Munster in the Heineken European Cup. If a player is tackled short of the goal-line, but can still reach over to ground the ball, or if their momentum carries them over, a try is awarded.

Try!

A try is scored when the ball is grounded under control in the area of the pitch called the in-goal area (see page 14). The try-scorer must put downward pressure on the ball as it touches the ground. The referee and touch judges watch carefully to see if the ball was held up by the defending team or if the player trying to score put a foot or any other part of his body out of the pitch before grounding the ball. Either of these occurrences will result in a try not being given. A penalty try is awarded when the referee thinks that a try would probably have been scored but was stopped by the other side breaking the rules. A penalty try's conversion kick (see below) is taken right in front of the posts.

MAD FACT

In rugby union's early days, conversion kicks were worth two points, but a try was worth only one point! A try's value changed to four points and in 1992, five points.

Conversions and Penalty Kicks

When a try is scored, the team can add two further points with a conversion kick. The target is between the goal posts, 5.6m apart, and over the 3-m high crossbar. The kick is taken in line with where the try was scored. Sometimes an attacker will keep on sprinting to score the try under the posts, giving their kicker an easier kick.

Penalty kicks are awarded by the referee and the team awarded the penalty can tap kick and then pass or run with the ball, kick to touch and play a lineout or take a kick at goal. If the kicker chooses to kick for goal, then the kick is taken where the penalty was awarded. With kicks on goal, the player has up to a minute to take the kick.

Drop Goals

A drop goal is scored in open play and is worth three points. Players usually drop kick the ball on the half volley – kicking the ball just as it bounces on the ground. Their aim is to send the ball away high enough to clear opponents and the goal crossbar. A team's kicker may stand further back than usual while his side has the ball. The kicker is said to be in the pocket, ready to receive the ball and attempt a drop goal.

Neil Jenkins keeps his eye on the ball as he makes a successful penalty kick for Wales.

S T A T   A T T A C K

In 1994, local South-east Asian rivals, Hong Kong and Singapore played an international match. The result was the highest ever international points total with Hong Kong thrashing Singapore 164-13!

All Time Test Match Points Scorers

Neil Jenkins	Wales	1,090
Diego Dominguez	Italy	1,010
Andrew Mehrtens	New Zealand	967
Jonny Wilkinson	England	914
Michael Lynagh	Australia	911
Matthew Burke	Australia	878
Ronan O'Gara	Ireland	742
Gavin Hastings	Scotland	667

Who is...

...Neil Jenkins?

Neil Jenkins holds the world record for points scored in international matches with a whopping 1,049 points for Wales and a further 41 in four tests for the British and Irish Lions. Playing for Wales from 1991 until retiring from international rugby in 2003, Jenkins played on for his club, the Celtic Warriors. In the 2003/04 season he notched up another world record, making 44 successful kicks at goal in a row for the Celtic Warriors.

⬤MOVING THE BALL

The rugby ball is moved around the field by players running with it, using their hands to pass it or their feet to kick it. Passing must always be sideways or backwards. Accidental forward passes see a referee award a scrum while intentional forward passes will see the referee signal a penalty to the other team.

Passing and Receiving

Apart from avoiding a forward pass, the passer must judge the game around him and the speed and direction of the player he intends to pass the ball to, known as the receiver. He must get the precise direction, timing and force of his pass absolutely right. A poorly timed, misdirected or badly thrown pass can lead to the receiver not reaching or overrunning the ball or an opponent intercepting the ball. Interceptions regularly lead to tries being scored.

The receiver of a pass also has to stay alert and cushion the ball with soft hands as it arrives, to collect it safely. Fumbling the ball so that it travels forwards is called a knock-on. Knock-ons are treated by the referee in the same way as forward passes. However, if a player fumbles the ball but catches it before it has hit the ground or another player, it is not a knock-on and play continues.

South Africa's Natasha Hofmeester looks to keep the ball alive by passing it as she is tackled by Samoa's Lorina Papalii.

Queensland Reds' Andrew Scotney charges down a kick from Chiefs' Danny Lee.

Kicking and Running

While passes always send the ball backwards or sideways, the ball can be moved forward through one player kicking it or running forward with the ball under control in their hands. Players tend to protect the ball from opponents by keeping it close to their chest. Top players running with the ball strive to stay aware of the position of team-mates as well as opponents. Try-scoring opportunities are sometimes wasted by players being greedy and not passing to a team-mate in a better position than themselves. There is a variety of kicks available to players, from short chips over an opponent to long punts which clear the ball a long distance upfield. Kicking gives away possession of the ball and kickers have to be careful. If their kick is charged down by an opponent and it bounces off the opponent and goes forward, the knock-on rule does not apply.

Tackled

Players run with the ball seeking to avoid being tackled by opponents. If they are tackled they must release the ball. They can do this by passing or offloading the ball to a team-mate. They can also do this by placing the ball on the ground, letting it go and moving away from it. A player slow to release or move away from the ball, trying to give his team-mates time to get the ball, will be penalized by the referee.

MAD ///// ///// FACTS

New Zealand All Blacks legend George Nepia caught the ball in a charity match in the 1950s, ran through a gap and scored a try. The only problem was that he was not playing full-back, he was refereeing the game!

PEOPLE ON THE PITCH

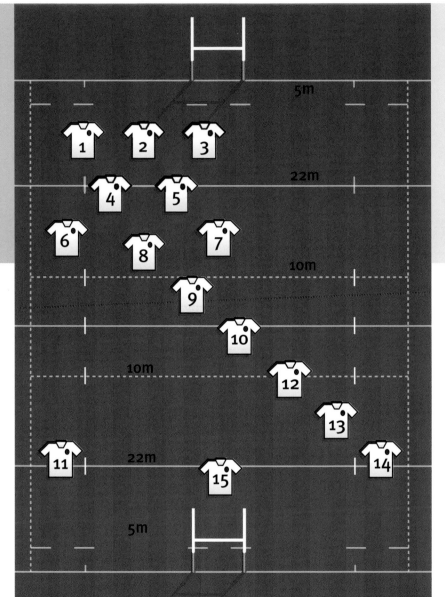

5m

22m

10m

10m

22m

5m

Rugby is played by teams of eight forwards and seven backs per side. The pitch is about 69m wide and 100m long. In addition to the 100-metre-long pitch area, there is an in-goal area at each end of the pitch that is 10-22m deep. The try line marks the front of the in-goal area and the dead ball line marks the back.

Forwards and Backs

The eight forwards' aim is to obtain possession of the ball and get it to their backs who are the main attacking and try-scoring force. Forwards used to be the slow heavyweights and backs the fast but lighter players. At the top level, this has changed. Most players are mobile, able to tackle and capable of interchanging roles.

1. Loose-head prop
2. Hooker
3. Tight-head prop
4. Second row
5. Second row
6. Blind-side flanker
7. Open-side flanker
8. Number 8
9. Scrum-half
10. Fly-half
11. Left wing
12. Inside centre
13. Outside centre
14. Right wing
15. Full-back

A rugby pitch with its markings and typical line-up of players. The pitch's boundaries are marked by the touchlines along the sides and the dead ball lines at each end. If a ball travels over the line, it is out of play.

Dash it

There are usually three sets of dashed lines on a pitch. The 10m line from the halfway line is used to judge that kickoffs have travelled the minimum distance. The 5m line close to the try line is the minimum distance from the try line that an attacking team can take a tap penalty or set a scrum, even if the offence occurred a few centimetres from the try line. Some pitches also have dashed lines running the length of the pitch 5m and 15m in from the touchlines. These lines help referees with lineouts (see page 17).

On the Line

The lines that border the pitch to the side – the touchlines – are considered out of play. A player who steps on to the touchline carrying the ball, for example, is in touch and out of play. When the ball travels on to or over the touchline it is out of play and the game is usually restarted with a lineout. The try line is considered part of the in-goal area, so an attacker grounding the ball on the try line has scored a try.

The weather can conspire to turn pitches, especially in the past, in to mudbaths. Here, members of the British Lions side in 1977 are covered head to toe in mud as they play New Zealand.

The 22

Running across the pitch 22m in front of each try line, the 22m line is involved in a number of key rules. For example, players inside their own 22-metre area can kick the ball directly out of play without the ball bouncing. If they are outside of their 22 and do that, the referee will award a scrum to the other team from where they took the kick. A 22m drop out is the way the game is restarted after the attacking side has failed to score a try, penalty kick or conversion and the ball has gone over the dead ball line or has been touched down by the defending team in their own in-goal area. The drop out is a kick taken from behind the 22m line.

THE FORWARDS

The eight forwards in a side have a series of tasks they must perform. They are expected to gain ground with the ball and be their side's most frequent and destructive tacklers. They are also responsible for securing possession of the ball in open play and at set pieces, such as the lineout and the scrum.

Scrums and Scrummaging

The scrum is a set piece awarded in a number of situations, including the ball being knocked-on or going forward. The eight forwards bind together in a formation of three in the front row, two in the second row and three in the back row. On the referee's signal, the two sets of forwards engage with the front rows of both sides, locking into position and the two props grab hold of their opposite numbers' shirts. The scrum-half feeds the ball straight down the tunnel that is formed between the two front rows. The hooker in the middle of the front row is expected to strike the ball with his foot, rolling it back to the feet of the player furthest back in the scrum, the number 8, who can control it or pick it up.

Australia's forwards use a scrummaging machine to work on their scrummaging technique. The players get their bodies low and in the ideal position to transmit power safely through the scrum. All players must stay bound together in this way until the ball has come out of the scrum.

The Front Row

The short, stocky heavyweights of a side, the tight-head and loose-head props are the scrummaging experts. The props help support their hooker, who must concentrate on connecting with the ball in the scrum while the opposition's hooker may also try to strike the ball and win a scrum 'against the head'.

Second Row

The two second-row players, also known as locks, are often the team's tallest men. They generate power in the scrum, enabling the props to do their job, and are also the key jumpers at the lineout. In addition, their height means they are expected to compete at restarts, where the ball is sent high into the air.

The Flankers and Number 8

Often the most mobile of the forwards, the flankers and number 8 have to perform all over the pitch, adding power in the scrum, competing or supporting in the lineout, harassing the opposition's scrum-half and fly-half and winning the ball in open play and carrying it forward. The number 8 is also the player who controls the ball at the back of the scrum.

Lineouts

The lineout is the main way of restarting the game when the ball has gone out of play along the touchlines. An equal number of forwards per side, between two and seven, line up with a 1m gap between the two rows. The row must be no closer than 5m and no further than 15m from the touchline. The team's thrower, usually the hooker, must throw the ball straight but can choose the timing, height and distance of his throw to target his own jumpers. The jumpers can catch the ball or pat it backwards to their scrum-half.

French second row forward, Sebastien Chabal, playing for Sale Sharks, shows great athleticism to bend backwards and catch the ball one-handedly in a lineout. A lineout jumper can be supported in his jump by the other forwards.

THE PLAY LINKERS

All players have to make decisions on a rugby pitch, from choosing the timing and angle of a run forward, to deciding when to commit to a tackle or when to pass or kick. The two players who usually handle the ball most, and therefore have the most decisions to make, are the number 9 and 10 – the scrum-half and the fly-half. These two players are responsible for linking the play of the forwards and the backs.

The Scrum-Half

The scrum-half is the first link between the forwards and backs. Scrum-halves need to be swift, accurate passers and many of the best, such as Wales's Dwayne Peel, France's Jean-Baptiste Elissalde and Australia's George Gregan tend to be small in stature but tough and fast over short distances. The scrum-half is usually the player who collects the ball at set pieces such as lineouts and scrums. He frequently passes to his fly-half although he may elect to kick or make a sniping run himself. In defence, he tries to chase and harass his opposite number into a mistake, as well as often forming the first line of defence.

STAT ATTACK

The all-time leading points scorer in the Tri Nations is New Zealand fly-half, Andrew Mehrtens. Of his whopping 328 points, only 5 points were from a try, the rest were kicks.

Understanding between a team's scrum-half and fly-half is crucial to success. Here, Ireland's scrum-half Peter Stringer passes to his fly-half Ronan O'Gara. The pair know each other's game inside out having played together many times for Ireland and even more for their provincial side, Munster.

The Fly-Half

Also known as the stand off, outside half or five eighths, the fly-half is the player the scrum-half most frequently passes to in set pieces, such as the scrum and the lineout, and also in open play. The fly-half is the team's most influential decision maker and is given the chance to direct a team's play by choosing what option to take. He has to time passes precisely, kick accurately and be able to break and run with the ball himself. Most of all he needs a cool head to make the right decision as opponents bear down on him.

More often than not, the fly-half is the team's place kicker. This means that he takes the team's kicks on goal – the penalty and conversion kicks. As a result, fly-halves of the calibre of Neil Jenkins, Andrew Mehrtens and Jonny Wilkinson dominate the all-time points scorer lists.

Dan Carter makes a trademark fast break, eluding the tackle of Olivier Milloud.

Who is...

...Dan Carter?

Dan Carter is arguably the most exciting young fly-half in the world. A dynamic runner, astute passer and accurate kicker, Carter plays for the New Zealand side the Crusaders in the Super-14 competition (see page 37) and made his debut for the All Blacks in 2003. His 16 tries, 98 conversions, 87 penalties and one drop goal mean that at the start of 2007 he had scored 540 points in just 35 Tests for the All Blacks. He was made the IRB's Player of the Year in 2005.

THE BACKS

The scrum-half and fly-half are two of the seven players in a team known as the backs. While the backs' main function is to attack, the modern game has put more and more emphasis on solid defence and the backs helping out the forwards in situations such as rucks.

Centres

Centres need to be good at both defence and attack. Strong and fast, they are expected to make tackles often on larger opponents, such as forwards, trying to break through. Passed to by their scrum-half or fly-half, centres look to make try-scoring opportunities by cutting through the opposition defence and passing or going it alone. Many tries are scored through the attacking efforts of top centres working together, such as the Irish pair, Gordon D'Arcy and Brian O'Driscoll.

Who is...
...David Campese?

David Campese became the 623rd Australian player in August, 1982. He sometimes played at full-back although his most successful position was as a brilliant, instinctive attacking winger. Campo quickly became a crowd favourite with his searing pace, trickery and high-stepping running style which often left tacklers grasping at thin air. In 101 caps for Australia over a 15 year long international career, he bagged a record 64 tries including six at the 1991 Rugby World Cup where he was the star of the tournament.

David Campese flies away down the wing on the way to scoring another try for Australia.

The Wingers

The real speed merchants in a team, the left and right wingers, play out wide. They look to be nearly at full pace when they receive the ball and get on the end of an attacking move. It is no surprise that many leading try scorers, such as Doug Howlett, David Campese and Rory Underwood, played on the wing. Top wingers try to perfect swerves and sidesteps (see page 31) so that they can cut in from the wing to gain support of team-mates or to go round the outside of an opponent. They must also work with their full-back and support him in defence.

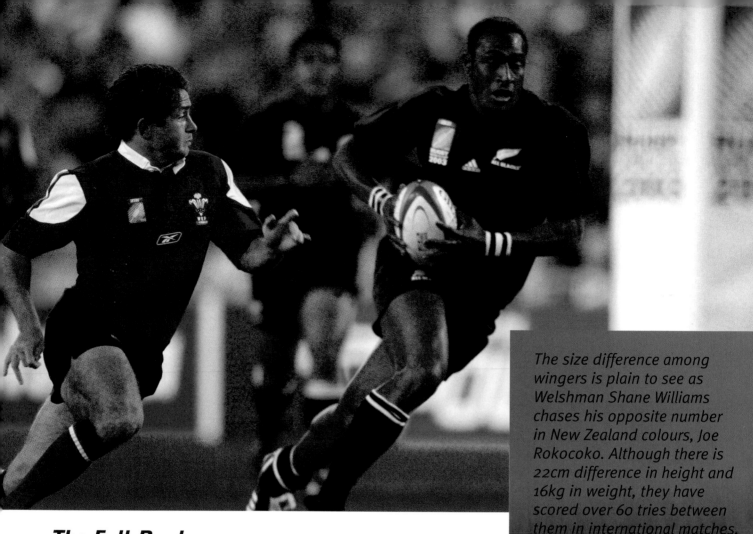

The size difference among wingers is plain to see as Welshman Shane Williams chases his opposite number in New Zealand colours, Joe Rokocoko. Although there is 22cm difference in height and 16kg in weight, they have scored over 60 tries between them in international matches.

The Full-Back

When a team's line of defenders is pierced by the opposition, the full-back is expected to make covering tackles. A full-back has to be comfortable at dealing with high kicks aimed at him by the opposition. A strong, elusive runner, a top full-back can be a potent attacking weapon as he has the freedom to roam and join in the attack at any point. Full-backs such as Chris Latham, Jason Robinson and Geordan Murphy are lethal try scorers.

MAD FACTS

Prince Alexander Obsolensky scored an astonishing 17 tries in a single game as a touring British team beat a Brazilian XV 82-0 in 1936.

Quick Feet, Quick Hands, Quick Reactions

Backs need lightning-fast handling skills and the decision-making ability to match the speed of their feet. Quick thinking can result in an opening which gains their side tens of metres of territory or even a try, but a rash decision can cost their side a penalty or try scored against them. An example of this is taking a quick tap penalty. When a referee signals a penalty for his side, a player can tap it to himself and run with the ball. Often, this can catch the opposition unawares and lead to a major attack. However, if the player is tackled and has no support, he can turn over the ball to the opposition.

THE OFFICIALS

A rugby union match is run by three officials – the referee and two touch judges who run the touchline. The touch judges aid the referee by reporting on if and where the ball or a player goes out of play. They also spot any foul play and judge kicks at goal. In major televised games, a television match official (TMO), known as the video referee, can be referred to by the referee to help rule on a try by watching television replays.

A Referee's Roles

Rugby union has some of the most complicated rules of any sport. Although a good referee must have a perfect knowledge of all the rules, this is only the start. Referees must be fit and have the stamina to keep up with play throughout the 80 minutes plus extra time, if it is played.

South African rugby union referee Andre Watson lies on the ground to get a closer look at a try as the Canberra Brumbies beat the Crusaders of New Zealand in the Rugby Super 12 final played in Canberra on 22 May 2004. The Brumbies defeated the Crusaders 47-38 to lift the trophy.

Referees must be neutral, work with the other officials and communicate their decisions by words and signals that are clear to players. Unlike in some sports, rugby referees are hugely respected by players who usually accept their decisions and do not argue. If they do argue with the referee, players are in danger of the referee penalizing them and, for instance, moving play forward 10m closer to their try line.

Referee signals

Try ⇨

⇦ Penalty

Knock-on ⇨

⇦ High tackle

Referees try to keep the game flowing. If an offence occurs, a referee may let the play continue if it is to the advantage of the team that did not offend. The referee signals that the teams are playing advantage and as the game continues, will either decide advantage is over or call the play back for the original offence.

Foul Play

Foul play comes in three forms: obstruction, unfair play, and dangerous play and misconduct. Obstruction is where one player unfairly prevents an opponent's movement by pushing or charging him or blocking a potential tackler from reaching the player with the ball. Examples of unfair play are when a team deliberately wastes time, throws the ball into touch to prevent opponents scoring a try, or repeatedly and unfairly slows the ball down out of the tackle. Kicking or punching an opponent or causing a scrum or maul (see page 27) to collapse are examples of dangerous play and misconduct.

Disciplining Players

Referees seek to defuse heated situations and sometimes may have a word with one or more players, usually with their captains present, to calm down a situation and warn players of their future conduct. Sometimes, though, foul play has to be penalized with more than a penalty or penalty try. Foul play can see a referee show a player a red card (sent off the pitch permanently) or a yellow card (sent off the pitch in to the sin bin for ten minutes). In both situations, the team has to play on with one less player.

S T A T   A T T A C K

Twenty players have received a yellow card at the first five Rugby World Cups. Only one player, Italy's Fabio Ongaro, has received two. Twelve players have received red cards. Seven of those were awarded to players from Canada (3), France (2) and Tonga (2).

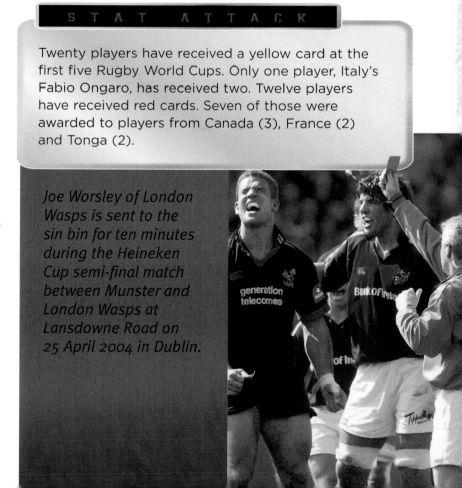

Joe Worsley of London Wasps is sent to the sin bin for ten minutes during the Heineken Cup semi-final match between Munster and London Wasps at Lansdowne Road on 25 April 2004 in Dublin.

TACTICS AND TECHNIQUES

The way a team decides to play is known as its tactics. Teams try to play to their strengths and away from their own weaknesses. They also try to target an opposition's weaknesses. Other factors that influence tactics include the pitch, weather conditions, players sent off or sin binned, and replacements.

Who is...

...Richie McCaw?

Richie McCaw was first appointed captain of New Zealand at the age of 23. He is one of the very best back row forwards in world rugby. Strong enough to prove a formidable defender, McCaw is sharp and decisive in gaining possession when the ball is loose and explosive with the ball in hand. He led the All Blacks to an unbeaten tour of Europe in 2006 and has 48 caps for his country, having scored nine tries.

New Zealand captain, Richie McCaw keeps his eyes on the ball as he catches a pass. Top players continue to drill their passing and catching throughout their careers.

Changing Play

A heavy, wet pitch and a heavy, highly effective pack of forwards may see a team play what is known as a tight game. Here, the team may keep the ball among the forwards for long periods, using drives, carries and kicks for territory and not passing the ball out wide to the backs very often. Other teams, with excellent attacking players and brilliant handling and fitness levels throughout the side, may prefer to play a more open, expansive game, passing the ball out to their backs and attacking in waves at every opportunity. Teams have to react to different situations as a game progresses. If an opposition full-back is struggling to catch high balls, the other team may choose to kick more often and launch high punts to test him to the limit. When a side is playing with a strong wind behind them, they may choose to kick long and pressure the other side close to their try line. If a team goes down to 14 or 13 players, their opponents may move their attacks back and forth across the whole width of the pitch, trying to find gaps in the defence.

Raphael Ibanez and the French forwards practise a lineout in training.

Coaching and Concentration

Hour upon hour on the training ground and in team meetings, coaches and players work hard so that their team's tactics and set pieces are well-drilled. However, all the best tactics and plans may go wrong if players do not concentrate for the full 80 minutes. Concentration and legs can fade in the crucial last 10 minutes, a period in which many tries are scored.

STAT ATTACK

Most Replacements at the Rugby World Cup (1987-2003)

Australia	94	Samoa	63
France	84	Scotland	58
New Zealand	78	Wales	57
England	70	Ireland	54
South Africa	65	Fiji	50

Replacements

Replacements may be temporary or permanent. Temporary replacements are used for up to 15 minutes when a player needs attention for a blood injury (known as the blood bin). Under the current laws, up to seven permanent replacements can be made in a match, depending on the competition. Once permanently replaced, a player cannot return. Some replacements are made when a player is injured, but often replacements are used tactically – to replace a tiring player with a fresh one or to change the style of play, for example, by replacing a more defence-minded fly-half or centre with a more attacking one or replacing a prop struggling in scrums.

DRIVING FORWARD

An important aim for the team with the ball is to gain ground. This can be defensive, to get the play away from their own try line, or it can be attacking, as the team with the ball strives to turn its possession into points.

Hard Yards

The forwards' role of getting the ball begins at kick-off and in 22 drop outs, where they chase and try to collect the high ball kicked to start or restart the game. It also extends to scrabbling about on the floor when the ball is loose, and trying to secure the ball so that their side can build an attack. Apart from obtaining the ball, forwards as well as backs are expected to gain ground with the ball in hand, making carries. A series of drives by forwards with the ball in hand can move a team deep into their opponent's half of the pitch. This works only if each time a player is stopped and tackled, he releases the ball cleanly and legally and in a way that a team-mate can pick up and continue the move forward.

Prop forward, Phil Vickery, rumbles forward with the ball as he drives at South African scrum-half Ricky Januarie and centre Jean De Villiers. In January 2007, England coach, Brian Ashton, appointed Vickery as captain of England.

MAD FACTS

Former England captain and back row forward, Laurence Dallaglio was a member of King House School Choir and sang at Andrew Lloyd Webber's wedding as well as on the Tina Turner record, *We Don't Need Another Hero!*

Rucks

A ruck occurs when the ball is on the ground and competing players from both teams are in physical contact. Rucks are complex and involve many rules. For example, only players staying on their feet can handle the ball in a ruck. Additional forwards can join a ruck providing they obey the rules and aim to drive over the ball and force their opponents back. This makes the ball available for the scrum-half to make a pass or for another forward to pick up and drive forward.

The England team drives forward in a rolling maul against Uruguay. Neil Back (right) has the ball tucked under his arm as he keeps in contact with his team-mates who all drive forward.

Mauls

Another way of gaining ground with the ball is the maul. Similar to a ruck, a maul forms after a tackle, but the ball is in the hands of a player and not on the floor and at least one player from each team closes round the player holding the ball. A rolling maul sees a number of players join a maul from the back; the ball is passed backwards to the player at the rear. He must stay in contact with team-mates as he rolls off the side of the maul, changing the direction as the maul drives forwards.

Although a rolling maul is slow-moving, once one gets going, it can be difficult to stop and can gain tens of metres of territory. It may also suck in more and more opponents so that when the ball finally comes out, there are large defensive gaps elsewhere on the pitch. If the rolling maul stops moving forward, the referee will let the team know that it has about five seconds in which to use the ball, otherwise the referee will award a scrum to the opposition.

MAD ///// ///// FACTS

Western Samoa's first international was against Fiji in 1924. The match was unusual in that it was played in a local park, and there was a tree in the centre of the pitch!

THE LINEOUT AND SCRUM

As set pieces in a game, the scrum and lineout are important ways of gaining the ball. If a team is struggling in either scrum or lineout, its opponents may target that set piece more often. For example, when awarded a penalty by a referee, a side can kick for goal, kick for touch or take a tap penalty and run. If they are confident in their lineout, they may gain territory with a kick for touch as they get the throw into the lineout. If their lineout is going badly, they may try to avoid tactics which result in that set piece.

Japanese (right) and South Korean (left) forwards form a scrum during a qualifying game for the 2007 Rugby World Cup. The narrower part of the pitch, if the scrum is not in the middle, is called the blindside. You will sometimes see the scrum-half collect the ball and run down the blindside.

MAD FACTS

Arnold Alcock was surprisingly capped by England against South Africa in 1906. The selection list was full of spelling mistakes. The selectors had meant to call up Andrew Slocock!

Scrum Tactics

A scrum ties eight players from each side in to a small area of the pitch, leaving large areas exposed to an attack from the backs. A scrum not too close to either touchline offers the team that puts the ball in generous areas of the pitch in which to attack. This team must aim to get the ball out of the scrum first. The opposing side will look to stand firm in the scrum and not concede any ground. If they can, the opposition forwards will seek to disrupt the scrum by turning it, or they will try to shove the scrum backwards. If a scrum is successful, the ball reaches the feet of the number 8. He has a number of options. He can leave the ball free for his scrum-half to pick up and pass, run with or kick. He can pick up the ball himself and power forward. Alternatively, he can control the ball at his feet as he and the rest of his pack push forward and drive the opposition back. This can gain valuable territory and, if the scrum drives over the try line and he or another forward grounds the ball, a pushover try is scored.

Lineout Play

Lineouts are practised a lot in training and teams will work on a number of different lineout jumps. These, they hope, are disguised from the opposition by the use of calls in code and by movement in the lineout. The team not throwing in the ball can jump and try to steal it at the lineout, but it has the disadvantage of not knowing the precise moment and aim of the throw.

Teams will often vary their lineout throws and change the number of players used in the lineout to keep the opposition guessing. If successfully carried out, a lineout close to the opposition try line can see the jumper hold on to the ball as he lands, and the other forwards form a driving movement around him, attempting to drive over the try line.

France's Aline Sagols tries to time her jump and stretch to intercept an Australian throw at a lineout during a 2006 Women's Rugby World Cup game.

ATTACKING PLAY

To attack well, teams look to move the ball fast and accurately. Players try to support their team-mate with the ball and ensure he has options for a pass just before, or as he is tackled. If he is tackled, team-mates try to ruck the ball rapidly so that the attack does not lose its momentum.

Running Lines

With the scrum-half and fly-half controlling many attacks, the other backs line up across the pitch. They seek to time their runs and choose a good angle or line for their run, so that they receive the ball and burst through the defence. A switch or scissors pass is sometimes used to change the direction of play. This is where the player with the ball is heading in one direction but turns at his waist and passes to a player running behind him in the opposite direction.

Creating Overlaps

An overlap is where there are more attackers than defenders – a situation which can lead to a try. Hard running by the player with the ball and supporting team-mates can leave one or two defenders isolated against three or more attackers. Repeated passing back and forth across the pitch can also generate an overlap.

A loop pass is another way to create an overlap. This is when a player passes the ball to a receiver and then runs around to become available for a pass himself. Performed at speed, the receiver becomes an extra attacker in the line, often creating an overlap.

England's Sue Day tries to choose a running angle that will take her past the French defence during the 2006 Women's Rugby World Cup. A good attacking line will aim for gaps in the opposition defence.

Individual Brilliance

Attacking backs are sometimes able to use their sprinting powers to beat an opponent. Players also use skills such as changes of pace, swerves and hand-offs, where the player uses an open palm to push an opponent away, in order to beat defenders.

Two of the most frequently used attacking skills are the sidestep and the dummy pass. A sidestep is where a player appears to be heading towards one side of a defender, but drives sharply off of one foot to head to the other side. The dummy is a convincing fake pass intended to lure the defender into moving one way to cover the pass. At the last moment, the player with the ball pulls the ball back in and tries to get past his unbalanced opponent.

In May 2006 in a match versus Georgia, Japan's Daisuke Ohata broke David Campese's record. In scoring his 65th international try, he became the world record try-scorer in internationals.

STAT ATTACK

Average Total Points and Tries per Match at Rugby World Cups.

Year	Points	Tries
1987	24.8	3.4
1991	19.8	2.3
1995	13.7	1.2
1999	56.1	5.6
2003	58.9	6.9

MAD FACTS

New Zealand player Howard Joseph was on his way to scoring a try in 1971 when he fell over a dog on the pitch and failed to score. New Zealand failed to win the match and lost their first ever series to the British Lions. Joseph never played for New Zealand again.

Kicks Ahead

There are a number of different kicks used to attack. All are a gamble, as the opposition may catch the ball in the air and the ball's bounce cannot be predicted. A player can chip kick the ball over a defender and try to collect it on the other side. Alternatively, he can try a low grubber kick where the ball travels end over end along the pitch, past defenders, for either the kicker or a team-mate to try to pick up. With the ball loose on the ground, a player can fly hack the ball forwards on the ground, chasing it like a football player and hoping to pick it up and run or, if it goes over the try line, to ground it and score.

DEFENCE AND TACKLING

A team's defence is all about stopping the opposition from scoring a try, or any other form of points, and getting the ball back in its possession. Players must be good tacklers but they have to work together as a unit for their team's defence to be successful.

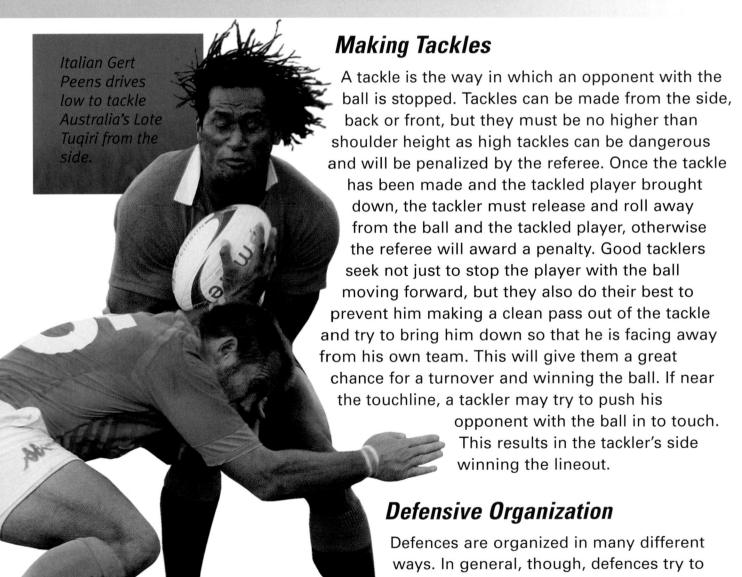

Italian Gert Peens drives low to tackle Australia's Lote Tuqiri from the side.

Making Tackles

A tackle is the way in which an opponent with the ball is stopped. Tackles can be made from the side, back or front, but they must be no higher than shoulder height as high tackles can be dangerous and will be penalized by the referee. Once the tackle has been made and the tackled player brought down, the tackler must release and roll away from the ball and the tackled player, otherwise the referee will award a penalty. Good tacklers seek not just to stop the player with the ball moving forward, but they also do their best to prevent him making a clean pass out of the tackle and try to bring him down so that he is facing away from his own team. This will give them a great chance for a turnover and winning the ball. If near the touchline, a tackler may try to push his opponent with the ball in to touch. This results in the tackler's side winning the lineout.

Defensive Organization

Defences are organized in many different ways. In general, though, defences try to advance forwards, cut out space and options for the opposing team and pressurise the attacker with the ball, trying to force him in to a mistake. Drift defence is one technique used by many sides.

It means that a defence moves or drifts as a unit towards the touchline that an opposition attack is moving towards. The aim is to reduce space where the ball and attackers are travelling and to ensure plenty of defensive cover. Players must concentrate, stay alert and be ready to move in all directions when defending.

Defensive Clearances

Possession of the ball is vital in rugby union. But when a team is close to its try line and under pressure, players may choose to kick the ball away to clear it from danger. A scrum-half may choose to clear, sometimes by kicking the ball over his shoulder. More often, he chooses to pass to the fly-half standing a little further back than usual, to give him a fraction of a second longer to make the kick. The fly-half tries to use a spiralling punt kick to send the ball vast distances upfield. Getting the ball into touch is preferred as it allows the team to regroup at a lineout. Their opponents are alert to this move and the flankers and other players may try to charge down the fly-half's kick.

Who is...

...Jason White?

Jason White is a Scottish back row forward and one of the fiercest and most effective tacklers in the modern game. White made his debut aged 21 for Scotland in 2000 in an epic 19-13 victory over England. He was appointed captain of Scotland in 2005. Part of Sale's 2005/06 English Premiership winning side, he was voted that league's Player's Player of the Year in 2006.

Scottish captain, Jason White, launches into a tackle stopping Welsh forward, Robert Sidoli in his tracks.

THE BIG COMPETITIONS

Top rugby players seek to test themselves against the best in the highest level competition possible. There is a large range of competitions at club and international level. In addition, many top players take part in Rugby Sevens matches where the spectators are treated to fast-paced action.

Who is...

...Waisale Serevi?

Waisale Serevi is considered the greatest Rugby Sevens player in the game's history The short, stocky Fijian possesses amazing balance and sleight of hand, skills which have enabled him to penetrate defences at will, delight crowds and score a hatful of tries. A five time winner of the Hong Kong Sevens and numerous other competitions, the magical Serevi has notched up an amazing 1,270 points in the IRB World Sevens Series and 297 points in the Sevens World Cup.

One-off Sides

The top-level rugby calendar is crammed with games. Officials have to balance issues concerning clubs and countries and the worries about player burnout and injuries from playing too many games. Often, the fixture list is added to by one-off matches featuring sides that are not regular clubs or national teams. For example, a Pacific Islanders team made up of players from Tonga, Fiji and Samoa toured Europe and played Ireland, Scotland and Wales in 2006. The most famous one-off side, the Barbarians, has no regular ground and players play by invitation only. Formed in 1890 to play exciting, attacking rugby, the Baa-Baas team often features star-studded line-ups from all over the globe.

Waisale Serevi shows his elusive running leaving France's Nicolas Carmona behind during an IRB World Series Rugby Sevens match. In 2006, Serevi became head coach of Fiji Sevens, masterminding their first ever IRB World Series championship.

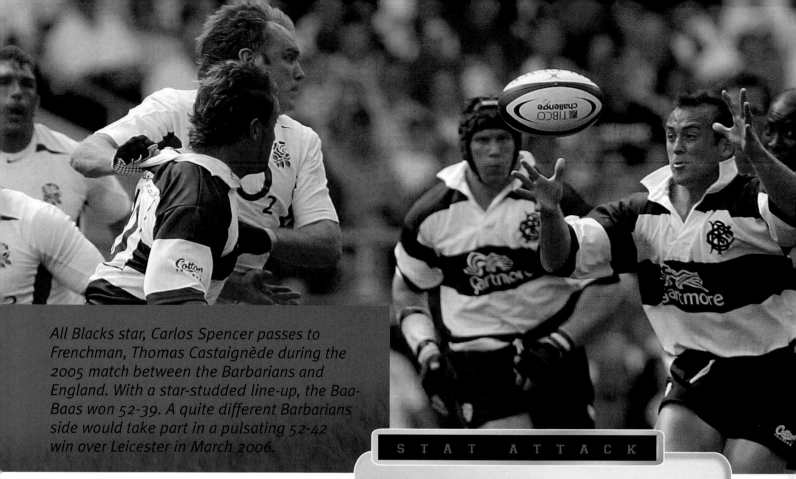

All Blacks star, Carlos Spencer passes to Frenchman, Thomas Castaignède during the 2005 match between the Barbarians and England. With a star-studded line-up, the Baa-Baas won 52-39. A quite different Barbarians side would take part in a pulsating 52-42 win over Leicester in March 2006.

Rugby Sevens

A simplified, stripped down version of the full game, sevens is a fast, exciting and, for the players, a lung-busting game played on a full-sized pitch. Games last seven or ten minutes per half. With just seven players a side, games are frequently open and high scoring and allow top players to exhibit amazing handling and attacking skills.

The most famous sevens tournament, the Hong Kong Sevens, is now part of the IRB Sevens World Series, while in recent years a number of other important competitions has emerged. Rugby Sevens was played at the Commonwealth Games for the first time in 1998, and with nations such as New Zealand, Australia, England and Fiji present, offers a high level of competition. Since 1995, four World Cup Sevens competitions have also been held with Fiji winning twice and New Zealand and England once.

MAD FACTS

The United States remain Olympic Champions at Rugby Union. The sport appeared at four Olympics, the last being the Paris Games in 1924.

CLUB, STATE AND PROVINCE

Club rugby is the core of rugby union. Big clubs can run dozens of teams at different age and ability levels. At the highest level, players are professional athletes paid a full or part-time wage by their clubs to compete in top leagues, cups and international competitions.

Felipe Contepomi aims to swerve around Toulouse's Gregory Lamboley in a 2006 Heineken Cup match. The Argentinian fly-half is a favourite with fans of his Irish Celtic League club side, Leinster. In 2005/06 he set a Celtic League record for the most points scored in a season – 276.

League Rugby

Many countries operate a league system, often with promotion and relegation between different divisions. In France, the Top 14 league is the highest level of competition. Since 1994, Toulouse, Stade Français and the 2005 and 2006 league winners, Biarritz, have won all the French league titles between them. The top league in England, the Premiership, consists of 12 teams playing one another at home and away and with a play-off system at the top, ending in a final to determine the winner. On three out of five occasions, the team that won the final match and was crowned the champion was not the side that had finished top of the league. The Celtic League was formed out of the Welsh-Scottish League, which ran in 1999 and 2000. It includes four teams from Wales, three from Scotland and four from Ireland, including 2005/06 champions, Ulster.

STAT ATTACK

Heineken Cup Finals

Year	Winner	Score	Runner-up	Score
1996	Toulouse	21	Cardiff	18
1997	Brive	28	Leicester	9
1998	Bath	19	Brive	18
1999	Ulster	21	Colombiers	6
2000	Northampton	9	Munster	8
2001	Leicester	34	Stade Français	30
2002	Leicester	15	Munster	9
2003	Toulouse	22	Perpignan	17
2004	Wasps	27	Toulouse	20
2005	Toulouse	18	Stade Français	12
2006	Munster	23	Biarritz	19

Super 12 and Super 14 Champions

1996	Auckland Blues
1997	Auckland Blues
1998	Canterbury Crusaders
1999	Canterbury Crusaders
2000	Crusaders
2001	Brumbies
2002	Crusaders
2003	Blues
2004	Brumbies
2005	Crusaders
2006	Crusaders

In the Cup

Cup knockout competitions exist in all rugby-playing nations, from the Air New Zealand Cup to South Africa's hotly contested Currie Cup. The format of some of these cups has changed over time. In England for example, the main cup competition which had been sponsored by Powergen, Pilkington and Tetley's over the years, was scrapped after the 2005 competition. In its place, was the Anglo-Welsh Cup, featuring the top 12 English clubs and the four Welsh provinces. The debut competition was won by London Wasps who beat Llanelli Scarlets. For club sides in Europe, the Heineken Cup competition, formed in 1995, is the premier competition. Teams from Ireland, Wales, Scotland, England, France and Italy gain a place in the cup based on their league position the previous season and they play matches which draw large crowds.

Super 12/14

In the southern hemisphere since 1996, the top level sees provinces or regions of the main countries compete in an international competition originally known as Super 12, because there were 12 sides in the competition. This became Super 14 in 2006, with the arrival of a fourth Australian side, the Western Force and a fifth South African team, Central Cheetahs. Each side plays the others once, with the top four placed sides playing semi-finals and a final to determine the champions.

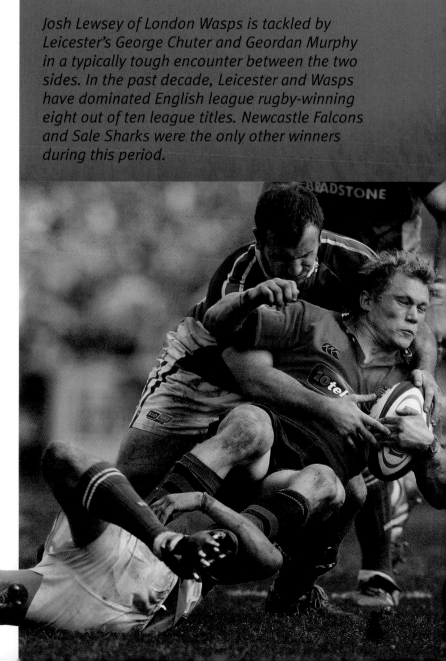

Josh Lewsey of London Wasps is tackled by Leicester's George Chuter and Geordan Murphy in a typically tough encounter between the two sides. In the past decade, Leicester and Wasps have dominated English league rugby-winning eight out of ten league titles. Newcastle Falcons and Sale Sharks were the only other winners during this period.

TOURS AND TESTS

Representing your country at Test level is the dream of many rugby players. Tests are sometimes played as one-offs but today are often part of a three-match series. In many cases, a trophy is played for. Among the most famous trophies are the Bledisloe Cup, donated in 1931 and won by the winner of the Test series between Australia and New Zealand, and the Calcutta Cup, for the winner of the England versus Scotland match.

Touring Sides

National teams go abroad on tours to play Tests. A tour usually involves some warm-up and midweek games against club or provincial sides and major international tests held on weekends. These are often keenly anticipated sell-outs. In recent years, autumn has seen the major southern hemisphere nations visit Europe, and national European teams depart in early summer to tour the southern nations. For European nations, touring Australia, South Africa and New Zealand has always been a tough test of their abilities. For 60 years (1896–1956), for example, South Africa never lost a Test series at home.

Who is...

...Jonny Wilkinson?

Jonny Wilkinson is England's record international points scorer, with 867 in just 55 caps. He was still a teenager when he went on the 1998 'Tour to Hell' where an inexperienced England side was thrashed by Australia and New Zealand. Obsessive in practising, Wilkinson became an incredibly accurate goalkicker but also an astute fly-half, capable of putting in thumping tackles. He remains the youngest player to reach 500 international points. The scorer of the famous drop goal which won England the 2003 World Cup, he has been on two British and Irish Lions tours.

After an absence from the England team of three years, Wilkinson made a surprise comeback in the first round of the 2007 Six Nations, where he scored 27 points and was made man of the match.

British and Irish Lions

The most famous touring side of all is a collection of players picked from England, Scotland, Wales and Ireland now known as the British and Irish Lions. The Lions have a long and illustrious history and their first tour, to Australia, took place in 1888. It is a great honour for a player to be picked for a Lions tour. Although the last tour to New Zealand under coach Clive Woodward was not a success, the Lions are usually extremely competitive, winning most of their non-Test matches and pushing their hosts in the Test series. Tours occur every four years with the next destination, South Africa, in 2009.

Women's Tests and World Cup

Although women had played rugby in clubs, universities and colleges for decades, it was not until 1982 that the first official international match occurred between France and the Netherlands. Nine years later, the first Women's Rugby World Cup was held in Wales. Since that time, the World Cup has helped boost the profile of women's rugby. The New Zealand women's team, the Silver Ferns, has won a hat-trick of World Cups with France perhaps the unluckiest side with four third place finishes in six competitions.

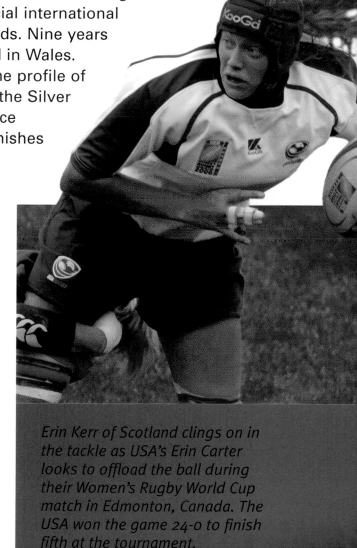

Erin Kerr of Scotland clings on in the tackle as USA's Erin Carter looks to offload the ball during their Women's Rugby World Cup match in Edmonton, Canada. The USA won the game 24-0 to finish fifth at the tournament.

STAT ATTACK

Recent British Lions Tours Test Results

1989 v. Australia	Lions won 2-1
1993 v. New Zealand	Lions lost 2-1
1997 v. South Africa	Lions won 2-1
2001 v. Australia	Lions lost 2-1
2005 v New Zealand	Lions lost 3-0

Women's Rugby World Cup

Year	Host	Winner	Runner Up
1991	Wales	USA 19	England 6
1994	Scotland	England 38	USA 23
1998	Netherlands	New Zealand 44	USA 12
2002	Spain	New Zealand 19	England 9
2006	Canada	New Zealand 25	England 17

SIX NATIONS AND TRI NATIONS

Most of the best national teams in the world play in one of two yearly tournaments – the Six Nations and the Tri Nations.

Six Nations

The oldest international rugby tournament in the world began in 1883 as the Home International Championship for England, Scotland, Wales and Ireland. France entered the fray in 1910 and Italy turned it from Five Nations to the Six Nations in 2001. The format of the championship has barely changed. Each side plays the others once, with home or away matches alternating each year. Two points are awarded for a win and one for a draw.

The drama and long history of the Six Nations sees games played out before

STAT ATTACK

Six Nations Championship [Recent] Winners

Year	Winner	Year	Winner
2007	France	1992	England
2006	France	1991	England
2005	Wales	1990	Scotland
2004	France	1989	France
2003	England	1988	Wales and France tie
2002	France		
2001	England	1987	France
2000	England	1986	France and Scotland
1999	Scotland		
1998	France	1985	Ireland
1997	France	1984	Scotland
1996	England	1983	France and Ireland
1995	England		
1994	Wales	1982	Ireland
1993	France	1981	France
		1980	England

France's Florian Fritz hands off Wales's Lee Byrne during a 2006 Six Nations match which France won 21-16.

packed crowds of passionate supporters every spring. All nations except Italy have won the tournament on a number of occasions. One of the most famous periods of dominance was that of the Welsh side which between 1969 and 1979 won a share of, or the championship outright, eight times. Winning all matches in a competition is known as performing the Grand Slam. Wales were the last Grand Slam champions in 2005. France achieved a Grand Slam the season before. If Wales, Scotland, Ireland or England beat the other three teams they are said to have won the Triple Crown.

The Tri Nations

The giants of the southern hemisphere's rugby – New Zealand, South Africa and Australia – lacked a regular tournament in which to compete until 1996 when the Tri Nations tournament began. The competition sees each side play the opposition twice. Four points are awarded for a win and two points for a draw (an event which has happened only once in the competition's history). Teams can also win a bonus point by either scoring four or more tries in a match or by losing by less than eight points in the game. The bonus point system is designed to encourage attacking play even if one team is so far behind that winning the game is almost impossible. The Tri Nations competition has produced some spectacular rugby and amazing games. One of the most impressive occurred in 1998, where South Africa were trailing the All Blacks by 18 points in the second half. They went on to score 19 unanswered points to win a thrilling match, 24-23. There is a lot of interest in expanding the tournament, with Argentina and the Pacific Islanders lobbying to be included.

Ruan Pienaar of the Springboks is tackled by New Zealand's Sitiveni Sivivatu during a thrilling 2006 Tri Nations match in which South Africa beat the eventual champions 21-20. In 2006, the number of games in the Tri Nations series increased with each side playing their opponents three times.

STAT ATTACK

- The 1973 Five Nations tournament ended with every match being won by the team playing at home. The end result was a five-way tie for the championship with each team on four points.

- The Six Nations trophy was first awarded in 1993. It is a large silver cup capable of holding 5 bottles of champagne. This became the normal practice for the winners, so much so that the inside of the cup became corroded and has had to be gold-plated!

THE WORLD CUP

Beginning in 1987, the Rugby World Cup is the sport's jewel in the crown. Held once every four years, the tournament attracts sell-out crowds and huge television audiences, as the best teams in the world battle to become world champions and lift the Webb Ellis trophy.

MAD FACTS

Australia beat South Africa in the 1999 semi final which went into extra time courtesy of Stephen Larkham's first ever drop goal in senior rugby! After winning the competition, the Australian side received a ticker tape parade back home with 150,000 fans present.

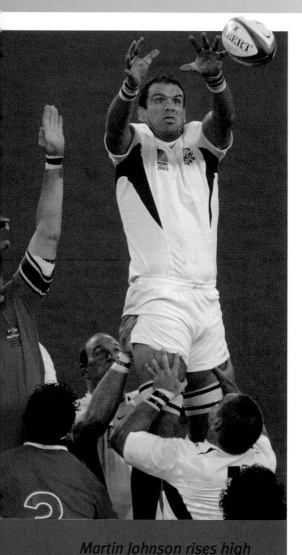

Martin Johnson rises high to catch a lineout ball during the 2003 World Cup final. England's captain was one of the players of the tournament. His inspired leadership and personal play drove England on to become world champions.

Qualification

The first World Cup saw 16 teams, including Japan, Zimbabwe and Romania, invited to attend the tournament. There was no qualification. But since then, a qualification competition is played. While the top nations in world rugby, the eight teams who reach the quarter finals of the previous World Cup gain a place automatically, others must compete for a limited number of places at the tournament proper. The number of nations involved in qualification has grown dramatically. Twenty-four nations were involved in qualifying for the 1991 World Cup, while qualifying for the 2003 tournament saw 92 countries play a total of 200 matches striving to qualify.

Amazing Action

Each Rugby World Cup has thrown up some astonishing performances both by individuals and teams. The 1987 tournament saw the unerring boot of All Black, Grant Fox notch up 126 points, a record still unbroken. In 1991 an almost unbeatable Australian defence conceded only three tries and, in David Campese, Australia had the star attacking player of the tournament, too. The 1995 Rugby World Cup was held in and won by South Africa. The Australian Wallabies were at it again in 1999, in a tournament increased from 16 teams to 20. This time the Australians let opponents score only one try against them while they racked up 24 points on the way to winning.

The 2003 competition featured 48 matches in 11 stadiums throughout Australia. It was the first time that the host nation was also defending champion. The tournament saw Australia rumble to the final along the way scoring a record 22 tries in a single match against Namibia. There, they met an England team that had beaten South Africa, Wales and France already. What followed was a tense, gripping tussle between two evenly-matched teams only decided by a last-gasp drop goal in extra time from Jonny Wilkinson. The 2007 Rugby World Cup was the first to be hosted in three countries with the majority of the games played in France but some in Wales and Scotland. In 2011 the tournament will be played in New Zealand.

STAT ATTACK

Rugby World Cup

Year	Winner	Runner Up
1987	New Zealand 29	France 9
1991	Australia 12	England 6
1995	South Africa 15	New Zealand 12 (aet)
1999	Australia 35	France 12
2003	England 20	Australia 17 (aet)

Top Individual Points Scorer per Tournament

1987 126 – Grant Fox (New Zealand)

1991 68 – Ralph Keyes (Ireland)

1995 112 – Thierry Lacroix (France)

1999 102 – Gonzalo Quesada (Argentina)

2003 113 – Jonny Wilkinson (England)

Arguably, the image of the 1995 Rugby World Cup was the Springbok captain Francois Pienaar receiving the Webb Ellis trophy from his country's president, Nelson Mandela. South Africa won a tense final against New Zealand. The game went into extra time with the scores level at 9-9. After both sides had traded three points, South Africa's Joel Stransky kicked a decisive drop goal.

WORLD CUP LEGENDS

The sport of rugby union has generated dozens of brilliant individual players, some of whom have been able to shine at the Rugby World Cup. Here are six players who have had a major impact on the tournament.

John Eales

In 1999, John Eales lifted the Webb Ellis trophy as captain of Australia, becoming one of only five players to have won two Rugby World Cups. The highly skilled 2m-tall second row forward captained his country a record 55 times and also notched over 170 international points, largely due to his role as a goal kicker, which is highly unusual for a forward. Eales retired from international rugby in September 2001.

Jonah Lomu

The New Zealand winger became the story of the 1995 World Cup as he rampaged through opposing teams, scoring seven tries in the process. Four of these came in an epic encounter with England which the All Blacks won 45-29. Lomu went one better at the 1999 World Cup with eight tries, the most any one player has scored at any World Cup. Struck down by an illness, Lomu had a kidney transplant in 2004 but battled back to play rugby at club level.

Serge Blanco

Although the Frenchman never won a World Cup, he will be remembered for scoring one of its greatest ever tries. With the score 24-24 in the last moments of the 1987 semi-final versus Australia, France were deep in their own territory. A magnificent attacking move, in which the ball went through 11 pairs of hands before Blanco finished off the move, sent France in to the final. Brilliant at full-back or as a winger, Blanco retired after the 1991 World Cup, having played 93 times and having scored a record 38 tries for his country.

MAD FACTS

The most points ever scored against a team at a World Cup is 145 by New Zealand in a match against Japan in 1995.

Gavin Hastings OBE

A veteran of three World Cups – 1987, 1991 and 1995 – Scotland's top Test Match scorer with 667 points was a brave and powerful full-back. Hastings endured heartbreak at the 1995 tournament semi-final against England where, with the score at 6-6, he missed an easy kick to win the game. But he can console himself with the fact that prior to the 2007 World Cup he is the record points scorer in the tournament with a whopping 227 points.

Jason Leonard OBE

The youngest prop forward to play for England when he debuted at age 21, Jason Leonard's 114 caps for his country are a record for a forward unlikely to be beaten for a long time. Able to play on both sides of the scrum, the hugely popular Londoner was a veteran of an amazing four out of the five World Cups held and part of the victorious 2003 side given an open-top bus parade through London. He captained England twice and on the second occasion, versus Argentina in 1996, scored his one international try.

> **S T A T   A T T A C K**
>
> **Shapes and Sizes at 2003 Rugby World Cup**
>
> **Heaviest player:** Joeli Veitayaki (Fiji): 136kg
>
> **Lightest Player:** Desmond Snyders (Namibia): 68kg
>
> **Tallest Player:** Luke Gross (USA): 206cm
>
> **Shortest Player:** Earl Va'a (Samoa): 166cm

Jason Robinson

A highly successful rugby league player, Robinson became one of the game's most successful converts from league to union. A dazzling runner who mixes searing pace with jinking ducks, weaves and sidesteps, Robinson could find his way through the most crowded parts of the pitch. Part of England's World Cup-winning side in 2003, Robinson announced his international retirement after 39 caps and 110 points in 2005. However, in 2007 he made a dramatic comeback in the Six Nations, scoring four tries in the tournament.

GLOSSARY

AET The abbreviation used in scoring for After Extra Time.

All Blacks The nickname of the New Zealand male rugby union team. The women's team is known as the Silver Ferns.

Blindside The narrower side of the pitch between the touchline and a scrum.

Cap The honour of making an appearance and playing for your full national team against another national team.

Conversion A kick awarded after a try which, if it sails between the posts, is worth a further two points.

Drill To practise a set-piece.

Drop out A type of kick used to restart a game of rugby union in many situations.

First team A country or club's top team.

Hat-trick To win three competitions or matches, usually in a row or to score three tries or drop kicks in a row.

Interception When a player of the defending team manages to catch the ball as it is passed by the other side.

Knock-on When the ball touches the hand or arm of a player and moves forward and touches the ground as a result.

Knock-out competition A competition where the loser of a match is knocked out of the tournament and the winning team goes on to play another game or is crowned champion.

Offloading Getting rid of the ball, usually by passing to a team-mate.

Open side The area bounded by the scrum and the touchline furthest away from the scrum.

Overlap An attacking situation where attackers outnumber defenders. Overlaps lead to an attack going around the defence.

Over-running When a player looking to receive the ball has moved too far ahead of the ball to collect the pass.

Possession When a player or team has the ball under control.

Replacement The term used in rugby for a substitute player.

Rugby league A different code of rugby. In rugby league, each team has 13 players. There are also different rules, for example, there are no lineouts in rugby league.

Selectors The people who pick the players for a team.

Set piece A term used to describe restart moves such as lineouts, scrums and drop outs.

Sidestep A sudden change of forward direction used by the ball carrier to get past a defender.

Spectators Another word for the fans who attend a rugby match.

Springboks The nickname of the South African male rugby union team.

Tap penalty A way of taking a penalty by kicking the ball to oneself. After the tap, the player can pass or run with the ball.

Test match A game between two national teams.

Wallabies The nickname of the Australian male rugby union national side.

WEBSITES

WWW.IRB.COM
The official website of the International Rugby Board. The IRB runs international rugby, including the World Cup. You can download a copy of the laws of the game from this website.

WWW.6-NATIONS-RUGBY.COM/ SIXNATIONS_ABOUTRUGBY.HTM
The official website of the Six Nations Championship, where you can find information on the latest matches and fixtures.

WWW.RFU.COM
The official website of the Rugby Football Union.

WWW.RUGBY.COM.AU
This website has all the latest news and information on Australian rugby.

WWW.PLANET-RUGBY.COM
An information-packed website with coverage of leagues, cups and national teams from all over the world.

WWW.ALLBLACKS.COM
The offical website of New Zealand's All Blacks. Log on to find out information on all the All Blacks players.

Note to parents and teachers:

Every effort has been made by the publishers to ensure that these websites are suitable for children, that they are of the highest educational value, and that they contain no inappropriate or offensive material. However, because of the nature of the Internet, it is impossible to guarantee that the contents of these sites will not be altered. We strongly advise that Internet access is supervised by a responsible adult.

INDEX